Reptilia Types

1. Crocodilians—alligators, crocodiles, and caimans
2. Snakes—these reptiles have no legs
3. Lizards—most lizards walk on four legs and many have long tails
4. Turtles and tortoises—these reptiles carry a protective shell
5. Tuatara—in a class by itself!

Even though reptiles include lots of different creatures, they all share these features:

- They're vertebrates, meaning they have a backbone.
- They're cold-blooded, which means they use the sun and air temperature to keep their body temperature even.
- They have dry scales, not hair or feathers.
- They breathe air with lungs, not gills.

Cold-blooded land animals like reptiles, frogs, and insects warm up in the sun or cool down in an underground nook.

Warm-blooded animals like mammals and birds produce their own body heat.

FEARSOME FANGS

Some reptiles eat only plants. Others prefer their meals more . . . well, meaty. Meat-eating reptiles gulp down animals as small as bugs and as big as buffalo. These predators sport all sorts of fearsome fangs. From an alligator's sturdy chompers to a cobra's venom-injecting teeth—all reptile teeth are designed to do two jobs: attack and eat!

Dental Details

Reptile teeth are as different as the types of reptiles out there. Here are just a few examples of what you might see in the wild.

Needle-like fangs: Tubed fangs or grooved teeth are designed to deliver *venom*, a poison that slows down or kills prey. Venom is modified saliva. An animal under the effects of venom usually can't move. This gives animals like snakes, who swallow their prey whole, time for a leisurely meal.

Spiny snares: Thin, hooked teeth are made for hanging on to quick-moving prey. Whether dinner is a slimy frog, a slippery fish, or a glob-like jellyfish, curved teeth prevent it from escaping. Boas have hooked teeth to hold prey while they coil their bodies around it.

Razor-sharp or pointed teeth: Great for piercing skin or hide. Serrated, or jagged, teeth can cut through thick material, like an insect's hard shell or animal bone. Check out the tuatara's jagged jaws for quickly cutting through a beetle's shell.

MORE TO IT THAN TEETH

Sure, reptiles have fabulous fangs. But they've also evolved other features that help them hunt. Here are just a few.

HIDDEN HUNTERS:

Many reptiles are ambush hunters, which means they use the element of surprise when they attack. Crocodilians like alligators, crocodiles, and caimans hide underwater, with only their eyes, nostrils, and ears above the surface. This focuses all of their senses on unsuspecting prey.

PURE POWER:

Camouflage and venom are helpful. But the surest way to slay prey? Strength. The massive green anaconda, the largest snake in the world, squeezes its prey to death before swallowing it whole. The saltwater crocodile has the strongest bite in the animal kingdom, chomping down with 3,700 pounds (1,680 kg) of force.

CUTTING CLAWS:

Many lizards have sharp nails that they use for climbing, hunting, and defense. The Komodo dragon slashes its prey with its claws during an attack.

SURPRISE STRIKE:

Reptilian predators stalk their prey, often leaping out when they're ready to attack. Venomous snakes and constrictors *strike*—which means they pull back their upper bodies and then launch themselves, fangs first, at their intended meal. The surprise attack combined with the force from the strike helps them get a good grip on their startled victims.

GILA MONSTER

SCIENTIFIC NAME:
HELODERMA SUSPECTUM

MONTHS BETWEEN MEALS

Named after the Gila River basin, where they were first discovered, Gila—sounds like *HEE-lah*—monsters are one of only a few lizards with venom in the world. These reptiles are black with orange, pink, or yellow splotches on their backs. For meals, Gila monsters snap up rodents, birds, and frogs, and gobble eggs they steal from nests. Because their desert habitats commonly reach 110 ° F (44 ° C), Gila monsters spend more than 95 percent of their lives underground to keep cool. How can they do this and not starve? Thanks to their fat-storing tails and their ability to digest *really* slowly, some scientists think these reptiles need to eat only three times a year!

LOCATION
SOUTHWESTERN UNITED STATES AND NORTHWESTERN MEXICO

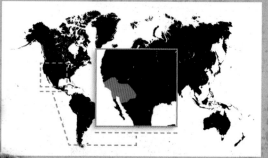

LENGTH
1.5 FT (0.5 M)

WEIGHT
4.5 LBS (2 KG)

6'0"

FANG FILE #1

Gila monsters have grooved teeth that hook backward to help them snag prey. These lizards release venom as they chew. The poison travels through the grooves in their lower teeth and into their next meal, making the prey unable to move.

GABOON VIPER

SCIENTIFIC NAME:
BITIS GABONICA

DID THOSE LEAVES JUST MOVE?

Surprise: it's a gaboon viper! This ambush hunter uses camouflage to disappear into the leafy rain forest floor. These large snakes are passive hunters, but when they strike, they're blindingly fast and accurate. Instead of striking and releasing, like other snakes, the gaboon viper sinks its teeth in and holds on—injecting more venom into its victims than any other snake. It's thought the venom from one gaboon viper bite could take down 30 people. With large, flat heads and horn-like flares on their noses, which grow as they age, these snakes look fierce. But despite their fearsome appearance and killer venom, gaboon vipers are known to be easygoing snakes.

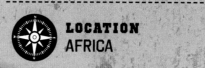

LOCATION
AFRICA

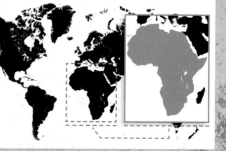

6'0"

LENGTH
4–7 FT (1.2–2 M)
WEIGHT
18–25 LBS (8–11 KG)

FANG FILE #2

Gaboon vipers have some fantastic fangs. In fact, with teeth measuring 2 inches (55 mm) long, gaboon vipers hold the Guinness World Record for the snake with the longest fangs.

BLACK MAMBA

🎓 SCIENTIFIC NAME:
DENDROASPIS POLYLEPIS

READY, SET, SLITHER!

If there were a race for snakes, the black mamba would win every time. These swift serpents are the fastest land snakes in the world, sprinting at speeds of up to 12.5 miles (20 km) per hour. Black mambas aren't black. They're actually gray-brown, which helps them blend in with their savanna habitats and sneak up on prey—small, furry mammals like hyraxes and bush babies. When threatened, these long snakes will raise their bodies off the ground and flare their neck flaps as if to say "Keep away!" If whatever—or whoever—doesn't listen, a mamba will strike not once (like most snakes), but many times, injecting deadly venom with each bite.

✴ **LOCATION**
EASTERN AFRICA

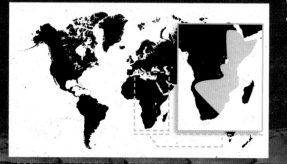

10

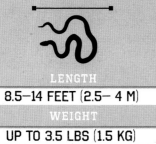

LENGTH
8.5–14 FEET (2.5– 4 M)

WEIGHT
UP TO 3.5 LBS (1.5 KG)

60"

DANGER!
GAUGE

10

FANG FILE #3

Black mambas are named for the bluish-black color of their mouths, easy to see when they bare their fangs. Black mamba teeth release some of the deadliest venom in the world, capable of taking down a person in 20 minutes.

AMERICAN ALLIGATOR

🎓 SCIENTIFIC NAME:
ALLIGATOR MISSISSIPPIENSIS

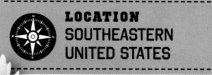

GREAT GATORS

Alligators live and hunt in freshwater rivers, swamps, and lakes. Their eyes, nose, and ears are all on top of their heads. This allows them to see, smell, and hear prey out of the water, while the rest of their body hides quietly beneath the surface. Gators have short legs, but their powerful tails make them swift and strong swimmers. Alligators hunt birds, frogs, and turtles in the water, and they'll snatch land animals that wander to the water's edge. Alligators have been known to eat animals as large as deer—and, sometimes, unlucky humans fall victim to a gator's carnivorous appetite.

✴ **LOCATION**
SOUTHEASTERN UNITED STATES

DANGER!
GAUGE

9

FEATURED FANG

FANG FILE #4

Gator teeth are shaped to chomp, not chew, and the powerful jaws of these heavyweight hunters hold as many as 80 pointed, saw-like teeth. Gator teeth fall out and are replaced often. A single alligator can go through 3,000 teeth in its life.

KING COBRA

SCIENTIFIC NAME:
OPHIOPHAGUS HANNAH

CHARMER OF A SNAKE

This famous cobra has one feature you'll recognize right away: its large flared hood. When angry or threatened, the cobra rears up, spreads its ribs, and flattens its body to display the hood. This strategy makes the snake look bigger than it actually is. Cobras can detect movement from a distance and can track movements by feeling vibrations in the ground. While these deadly snakes can inject venom powerful enough to topple an elephant, they prefer to dine on other snakes.

LOCATION
INDIA, SOUTHERN CHINA, AND SOUTHEAST ASIA

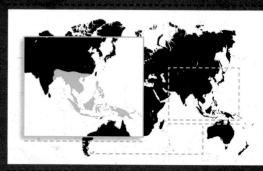

6'0"

LENGTH
13–18 FT (3.9–5.4 M)
WEIGHT
UP TO 20 LBS (9 KG)

FANG FILE #5

With their needle-like teeth, king cobras inject venom that makes their prey unable to move. Cobras swallow their food whole. Their backward-facing teeth help keep the meal moving in the right direction—toward the stomach.

RATTLESNAKE

Rattlesnakes are named for their noisy rattle-tipped tails. The rattle is made up of segments of hard keratin—the same stuff that your fingernails and toenails are made of. The keratin segments, which look like rings, are left over after the snake sheds its skin. Every time the rattlesnake sheds its skin, it gets another "ring." When the rattler shakes its tail, the rings knock against each other. What's the point of all that racket? To warn predators like king snakes, roadrunners, and hawks to back away unless they want to be bitten.

SCIENTIFIC NAME:
CROTALUS SPP. AND SISTRURUS SPP.

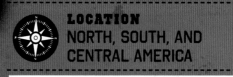

LOCATION
NORTH, SOUTH, AND CENTRAL AMERICA

6'0"

LENGTH
1 FT TO 5–8 FT (0.3 TO 1.4–2.4 M)
WEIGHT
4–10 LBS (1.8–4.5 KG)

FANG FILE #6

Most of the time, a rattlesnake's two curved, venom-filled fangs are tucked away against the roof of its mouth. When needed, the fangs flip down into striking position. The size of a rattler's fangs depends upon the size and species of the snake.

GREEN IGUANA

SCIENTIFIC NAME:
IGUANA IGUANA

GOOD-BYE, TAIL

Green iguanas, also known as common iguanas, live in the treetops of Central and South America. Their feet have five long claws used for gripping branches, and their long tail helps them balance. But iguanas are not only comfortable in the trees. They're quick on the ground and in the water, where they can swim underwater for up to 30 minutes. For defense, an iguana whips its agile tail at attackers. If a predator catches the lizard by its tail, the iguana detaches itself—leaving part of the still-wiggling tail, and the puzzled predator, behind. The tail will grow back, but until it does, the iguana is especially vulnerable to other attackers.

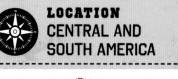

LOCATION
**CENTRAL AND
SOUTH AMERICA**

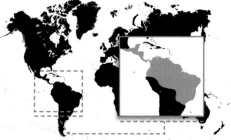

LENGTH
UP TO 6.5 FT (2 M)

WEIGHT
11 LBS (5 KG)

6'0"

DANGER!
GAUGE

1

FANG FILE #7

Iguanas use their razor sharp teeth to rip
into . . . fruits, leaves, and other vegetation!
Iguanas are primarily herbivores and nibble
away at the green stuff during the day.

EMERALD TREE BOA

HANGING AROUND

At the end of an emerald tree boa's body is a *prehensile* (pre-HEN-sul) tail, which means it's specially designed to coil and grip. This is a handy adaptation for a snake that lives in trees! In fact, it's very rare to see one of these snakes on the ground. You'll usually find them coiled around a branch in a loop with their head in the middle. Emerald tree boas are excellent hunters, feeding on rodents and birds that live in trees. Like many snakes, they have heat-sensing organs called pits, but emerald tree boas have more pits around their faces than most snakes do. The sensors show the snake a heat-image of its prey.

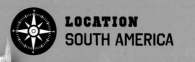

LOCATION
SOUTH AMERICA

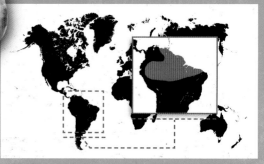

20

6'0"

LENGTH
UP TO 10 FT (1.8 M)
WEIGHT
ABOUT 3 LBS (1,500 G)

FANG FILE #8

Although their primary diet is rodents, emerald tree boas also prey on birds, sometimes even snapping them up in flight. The boa's long, curved teeth sink through the feathers and grip tightly, while the snake coils its body around the bird and squeezes tight. Once the animal stops breathing, the boa swallows it whole.

INLAND TAIPAN

SCIENTIFIC NAME:
OXYURANUS
MICROLEPIDOTUS

THE SHY BUT FIERCE SNAKE

Known for its super-strong venom, the inland taipan, also called "fierce snake," is one of the most feared snakes in the world. Luckily, people don't cross paths with it often: It's a shy snake that spends lots of time underground in the clay-filled floodplains of Australia. The taipan's body color changes depending on the time of year—from sandy brown in summer to dark brown in winter. Scientists think this helps the snake regulate its body temperature. The dark color helps it absorb more light and warm up faster in winter, and the lighter color helps keep it cooler in the summer.

LOCATION
AUSTRALIA

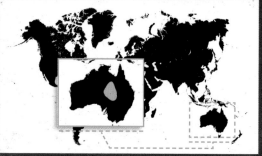

6'0"

LENGTH
7 FT (2 M)

WEIGHT
UNKNOWN

FANG FILE #9

The inland taipan is considered by many to be the world's most venomous snake. It's estimated that a single bite from this snake's fangs will deliver enough venom to kill 100 people—yet no human death from a taipan has ever been recorded. It usually goes after its favorite food, the long-haired rat.

BLACK CAIMAN

PROTECTED

SCIENTIFIC NAME:
MELANOSUCHUS NIGER

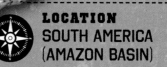

A CROCODILE COUSIN

Black caimans most resemble the American alligator. The largest of all caimans, these huge crocodilians are known for their large eyes and black scales. Young black caimans sport bright yellow stripes and spots, but these colorful markings fade as the reptiles age. Black caimans are the second largest predators (green anacondas are longer) in the freshwater rivers, lakes, and flooded plains of the Amazon. Once overhunted for their unique black skins, these crocodilians became a protected species and restrictions were placed on hunting them. It looks like these efforts have helped, and black caiman populations are once again growing.

LOCATION
SOUTH AMERICA
(AMAZON BASIN)

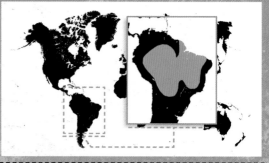

6'0"

LENGTH
UP TO 16 FT (5 M)
WEIGHT
800 LBS (363 KG)

FANG FILE #10

Like other crocodilians, the black caiman has a broad snout filled with about 76 teeth. Adults typically eat fish, like catfish and even dangerous piranhas, but they'll also chow down on capybaras, which are large, dog-size rodents that live in the Amazon.

TUATARA

A "LIVING DINOSAUR"?

What's so special about the tuatara? Plenty! It looks like a lizard, but it's actually the only living descendant of prehistoric reptiles called Rhynchocephalia. Every other type of this reptile went extinct 60 million years ago. That's why some people call the tuatara a "living fossil" or "living dinosaur." Another special feature is the third eye on the top of its head. Scientists think it might help the animal adjust to changes in weather and seasons. As the tuatara ages, the eye is eventually covered over by scales. These reptiles may live as long as 100 years.

SCIENTIFIC NAME:
SPHENODON PUNCTATUS

LOCATION
NEW ZEALAND

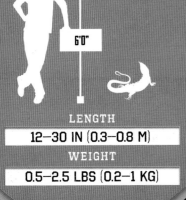

6'0"

LENGTH
12–30 IN (0.3–0.8 M)
WEIGHT
0.5–2.5 LBS (0.2–1 KG)

DANGER!
GAUGE

0

FANG FILE #11

While many reptiles have teeth that fall out and are replaced, tuataras' teeth are fused to their jawbones. This means they can't be replaced when they're worn down or broken. As tuataras get older, they go from eating hard-shelled beetles to softer foods like worms and grubs. A tuatara has two rows of teeth on the top jaw and one row on the bottom. The bottom row fits perfectly between the top two rows when the mouth is closed.

BUSH VIPER

SMALL BUT TOUGH

The deadly bush viper lurks in the rain forests of Africa, its green color blending into its surroundings. This big-eyed snake has rough scales to help it grip the trees it climbs while hunting. Its strong and flexible tail helps it hold on to branches. Bush vipers are patient ambush hunters. They will stalk prey slowly, staying still for a very long time before striking.

SCIENTIFIC NAME:
ATHERIS SQUAMIGERA

LOCATION
EAST, WEST, AND CENTRAL AFRICA

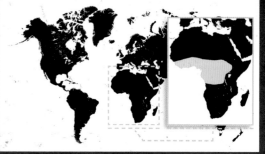

LENGTH
20–31 IN (50–80 CM)

WEIGHT
UNKNOWN

6'0"

DANGER! GAUGE

6

FANG FILE #12

This small snake packs a powerful, venom-filled bite. Its tube-like fangs are connected to a gland that pumps venom into prey. The fangs are retractable (fold back) so the snake doesn't bite itself. Bush vipers are nocturnal (nok-TUR-nul) hunters—preying on animals that come out at night, like frogs, rodents, lizards, and small mammals.

RED SPITTING COBRA

SCIENTIFIC NAME:
NAJA PALLIDA

SLITHERING SPITTERS

When threatened, a red spitting cobra will lift its body off the ground and puff out its cobra hood, just like its other relatives in the cobra family. But this cobra has another handy move to make animals back off: It spits stinging venom into the eyes of predators—hurting them at the least and blinding them at most. Scientists studying these snakes find that they hit their spit-targets most of the time. You might think this poisonous squirt would be helpful in hunting, but experts say spitting is used only for defense, to help the snake protect itself.

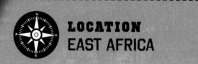

LOCATION
EAST AFRICA

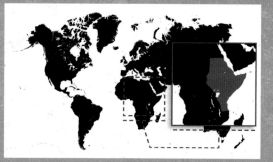

LENGTH
2.5–4 FT (0.7–1.2 M)
WEIGHT
UNABLE TO VERIFY

FANG FILE #13

Despite their name, spitting cobras don't actually spit—they're really shooting venom out of tubes in their fangs. The spray can reach up to 8 feet (2.4 m). Duck!

31

INDIAN GHARIAL

SCIENTIFIC NAME:
GAVIALIS GANGETICUS

A BIT NOSY

The Indian gharial is similar to its alligator and crocodile cousins, but with one very noticeable difference: a super-long, super-thin snout lined with pointy teeth. Its streamlined jaw allows the gharial to move its mouth around quickly in water, which makes catching fast-swimming fish a snap. Male gharials grow rounded bulbs at the end of their snouts, called a ghara, which is the Indian word for "pot." Scientists think the gharas help male gharials communicate with females by producing a loud buzz.

LOCATION
INDIA, BANGLADESH, BHUTAN, NEPAL, AND PAKISTAN

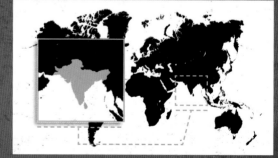

LENGTH
11–15 FT (3.5–4.5 M)
WEIGHT
350–399 LBS (159–181 KG)

6'0"

3

FANG FILE #14

An Indian gharial has about 110 needle-like teeth lining its narrow jaws. Like its jaws, the gharial's teeth are perfectly adapted for spearing slippery fish, this crocodilian's favorite food.

BOOMSLANG

BEAUTIFUL BOOMSLANG

Big-eyed with beautiful green-and-brown markings, the boomslang was once considered a harmless tree-dwelling snake. It wasn't until the famous herpetologist (her-puh-TOL-uh-gist)—that means snake scientist—Karl P. Schmidt was accidentally bitten and later died from the venom that people figured out that boomslangs were deadly. Boomslangs find tree chameleons particularly tasty and will stalk them for a long time before attacking. If a boomslang thinks it's been spotted, it will freeze, usually with the front of its body extended off the tree. They'll even sway slowly, just like a tree branch moving in the breeze.

SCIENTIFIC NAME:
DISPHOLIDUS TYPUS

LOCATION
SUB-SAHARAN AFRICA

6'0"

LENGTH
3–6 FT (0.9–1.8 M)
WEIGHT
0.5–1 LBS (0.2–0.5 KG)

DANGER!
GAUGE

7

FANG FILE #15

Boomslangs are unusually deadly for a tree snake. They deliver
venom by grooved fangs at the back of their mouths, which
means they have to open their mouths really wide to attack.

COPPERHEAD

STRIKE FIRST

Copperheads have keeled scales, which means each scale has a ridge on it. This makes the snake rough to the touch. Many snakes will display warning behavior when threatened—like a rattlesnake's rattle or a black mamba's open and hissing mouth. But copperheads strike first! So give a copperhead lots of room if you encounter one in the wild. Young copperheads have a vivid yellow tail. Young copperheads wiggle their tails to mimic worms, attracting delicious bugs to eat. The yellow color fades with age, and as the copperheads' diet changes.

LOCATION
NORTH AMERICA,
FROM FLORIDA PANHANDLE UP TO MASSACHUSETTS
AND THEN WEST TO NEBRASKA

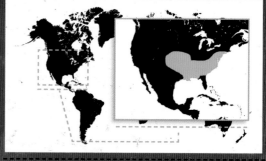

LENGTH
UP TO 31 IN (76 CM)
WEIGHT
1 LB (0.31 KG)

DANGER!
GAUGE

7

FEATURED FANG

FANG FILE #16

Baby copperheads are born with fangs, and their venom is as potent as that of an adult. Copperheads' fangs grow with the snake: the bigger the copperhead, the bigger the teeth. Favorite foods include birds, lizards, frogs, and large insects.

NILE CROCODILE

SCIENTIFIC NAME:
CROCODYLUS NILOTICUS

CARING CROCS

A relative of the American alligator, the Nile crocodile is the largest croc in Africa. These huge reptiles can be found in lakes and rivers. Though their diet is mostly fish, they've been known to take a bite out of anything within chomping distance—including birds, zebras, small hippos, wildebeests, other crocodiles, and even unlucky humans. But these toothy crocodilians aren't all bite. They're also very caring parents. Most reptiles leave their eggs and babies on their own, but Nile crocodiles guard their nests, help their babies hatch, and even keep an eye on them until they're about two years old. Isn't that sweet?

LOCATION
AFRICA

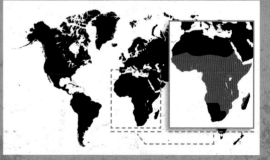

6'0"

LENGTH
16–20 FT (5–6 M)

WEIGHT
500–1600 LBS (227–725 KG)

FANG FILE #17

The Nile crocodile's powerful jaws house 68 pointed teeth. The muscles that close a croc's mouth can clamp down with thousands of pounds of force. But the muscles that open those jaws are so weak that a rubber band can keep the croc's mouth shut.

GREEN ANACONDA

SCIENTIFIC NAME:
EUNECTES MURINUS

SSSSSUPERSIZED SNAKE!

The green anaconda is the biggest snake in the world! Weighing more than an adult lion and longer than a giraffe is tall, these colossal constrictors have an appetite for big prey. Wild deer, wild pigs, caimans, and even jaguars all make tasty meals for green anacondas. These hefty members of the boa family don't need venom to kill their prey. Instead, they coil their enormous bodies around an animal to restrict blood flow. Then they swallow their meal whole. Green anacondas slither in swamps, where they can move quickly through water to snap up animals that come to the edge for a drink.

LOCATION
SOUTH AMERICAN RAIN FORESTS

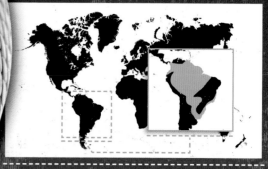

LENGTH
UP TO 30 FEET

WEIGHT
UP TO 550 LBS (250 KG)

6'0"

DANGER! GAUGE

7

FANG FILE #18

Green anacondas have four rows of hooked teeth on the tops of their mouths and another two on the bottom. The hooks help them latch on to prey while they coil their bodies for the kill. Their jaws are connected to stretchy tissues that allow anacondas to open really wide and swallow prey whole.

41

KOMODO DRAGON

ENDANGERED!

SCIENTIFIC NAME:
VARANUS KOMODOENSIS

THAR BE DRAGONS

The largest—and most deadly—lizard in the world is the Komodo dragon. Found only on five islands in Indonesia, these top predators attack other lizards, pigs, deer, water buffalo, and—sometimes—people. Dragons use their forked yellow tongues to smell, and they can catch the scent of a dead or bleeding animal up to 6 miles away. Ambush hunters that rely on surprise attacks, dragons stalk their prey, camouflaged by their skin color. When the animal being tracked least expects it, the dragon lunges, shredding with its long, sharp claws and chomping with its terrible serrated teeth.

LOCATION
INDONESIA

LENGTH
8–10 FT (2.5–3 M)
WEIGHT
UP TO 154 LBS (70 KG)

6'0"

FEATURED FANG

FANG FILE #19

Komodo dragons have 60 curved and jagged teeth measuring as long as 1 inch (2.5 cm). The lizard uses its powerful jaws and neck muscles to help it rip chunks out of prey. If a dragon's awesome chomp doesn't kill prey immediately, its venom slowly will.

LEATHERBACK SEA TURTLE

ENDANGERED!

SCIENTIFIC NAME:
DERMOCHELYS CORIACEA

TREMENDOUS TURTLE

The leatherback sea turtle is the largest living turtle. Most turtles have hard shells, but not these big swimmers. They have soft, rubbery, leather-like backs between stiff ridges. Leatherbacks travel long distances and can be found in oceans worldwide. But even with their wide range, they are endangered. Out of 1,000 hatchlings, only one baby turtle will grow to be an adult. One big danger to leatherbacks is plastic pollution. In the water, a floating plastic bag looks like the turtles' favorite food: jellyfish. The plastic bags can suffocate or choke a turtle. There are only about 50,000 nesting females left in the world.

LOCATION
ATLANTIC, PACIFIC, AND INDIAN OCEANS; MEDITERRANEAN SEA

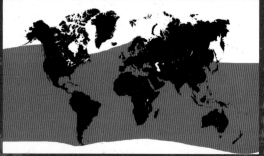

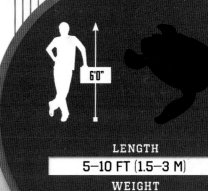

LENGTH
5–10 FT (1.5–3 M)
WEIGHT
800–2,000 LBS (362–900 KG)

6'0"

FANG FILE #20

Do turtles have teeth? Not exactly. Huge leatherbacks eat mostly jellyfish, which don't have a lot of protein or vitamins. So they need to eat a lot every day—over 500 lbs (227 kg) for an average leatherback. They keep those slippery suppers down thanks to their papillae (puh-PIL-ee). These spiny cartilage prongs line the leatherback's mouth, throat, and esophagus down to the gut, keeping the jellies from slipping back out when the turtle swallows.

45

WHAT'S FOR DINNER?

When it comes to prey, reptiles have appetites that range from enormous to tiny. Whether it's a bug buffet, a lizard lunch, a buffalo banquet, or a seaweed salad, there's a reptile out there ready to gobble it up.

CRUSH!

The southern brown egg-eating snake has eggs for breakfast . . . and lunch . . . and dinner! This nonvenomous African species feeds only on bird eggs. The snake gulps the egg whole, crushing the shell as the egg moves down its throat.

SNIP!

The Galápagos tortoise munches on greens like grass, leaves, berries, and lichen. They especially enjoy cacti. Thanks to specially adapted energy and water storage systems in their bodies, these big guys can go for a year between meals if they need to.

GULP!

The golden tree snake uses its mild venom to slow down fast-moving prey. The venom stops the would-be meal, like this butterfly lizard, in its tracks. Then the slithering stalker gulps its dinner whole.

CRUNCH!

Grasshoppers make a tasty treat for a bearded dragon. These lizards are not picky eaters. When they're hungry, plants, insects, spiders, small rodents, and even other lizards will do.

YIKES!

Crocodiles are ambush hunters. They sneak up on their prey and grab it, holding tight with sharp teeth and powerful jaws. This wildebeest had an unwelcome surprise when it stopped by a watering hole for a drink.

![becker&mayer! BOOK PRODUCERS]

Published by becker&mayer! LLC
11120 NE 33rd Place, Suite 101
Bellevue, WA 98004
www.beckermayer.com

Author: L. J. Tracosas
Designer: Sam Dawson
Editor: Betsy Henry Pringle
Photo researcher: Farley Bookout
Product developer: Peter Schumacher
Production coordinator: Tom Miller
Product sourcing: Jen Matasich

10 9 8 7 6 5 4 3 2 1
ISBN: 978-1-60380-392-2
Made in China. 2016.07.
15754